"Every man must have a dream..."

Liverpool Express, 1976

THE sizzling Seventies gave Merseyside a change of direction after the swinging Sixties.

Life went on in Liverpool, despite the end of the Beatles. Glam rock, punks and disco babes replaced the mop heads and hippy chicks. The fashions were all about big heels, flares and tank tops.

Men were getting their hair permed – including more than a few footballers. Everton landed the league title in 1970 and it was the decade when Liverpool FC finally came of age as a true European force.

It was a golden era for television, when Scouse talent like Leonard Rossiter, Tom O'Connor, Carla Lane and Eddie Braben proved to the nation why our reputation for humour was no joke.

In 1977 there was dancing in the street as folk turned out to celebrate the Silver Jubilee with a right Royal knees-up and parties in every neighbourhood.

Meanwhile in Mathew Street, the spirit of punk was rebelling against everything and anything.

Storm clouds had already gathered over the industrial scene and more than 92,000 redundancies were announced, culminating in the strike-driven 'Winter of Discontent' in 78/79.

The Seventies might have become the decade to get down and feel good, but it was also an ugly era, dominated by industrial strikes, terrorism and the grim reality of the bomb and the bullet.

Once there was a time when women were seen as little more than mothers and housewives. In 1979 Britain elected its first female Prime Minister.

Words: Vicky Andrews, Peter Grant, Colin Hunt

Photography: Liverpool Daily Post and Echo Archives, image of John Lennon courtesy of Mirrorpix

Picture Research: Leslie Rawlinson, Brian Johnston

Design and Layout: Zoe Bevan, Colin Harrison, Vicky Andrews

Published by: Trinity Mirror Merseyside, PO Box 48, Old Hall Street, Liverpool L69 3EB

Printed by: Pensord, Tram Road, Pontllanfraith, Blackwood NP12 2YA

ISBN: 978-1-906802-19-6

John Lennon
pictured in 1970

THE END OF THE BEATLES

THE 1970s in Liverpool began with the end of an era – Beatlemania was finally laid to rest.

Paul McCartney marked the end on April 10, 1970, when he announced he was leaving the Beatles. It was the end of the greatest pop group in history. McCartney said the split was the result of "personal differences, business differences, musical differences – but most of all because I have a better time with my family."

The Beatles had appeared to be drifting apart as members pursued individual projects. McCartney's High Court writ to dissolve "the business carried on . . . as the Beatles & Co" coincided with the announcement of his new LP, called McCartney, which he made with his wife Linda.

Asked if the pair would become "the next John and Yoko", Paul replied: "No, we'll be the first Paul and Linda."

Insiders blamed the split on the growing tension between McCartney and his songwriting partner John Lennon. Paul said he enjoyed working solo and that although he still loved John, he couldn't foresee any future for the Lennon-McCartney partnership.

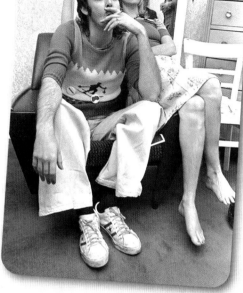

NATIONAL HEADLINES

1 January The half crown coin ceases to be legal tender.

22 January A Boeing 747 lands at Heathrow Airport, the first jumbo jet to land in Britain.

9 May In Washington DC, 100,000 people demonstrate against the Vietnam War.

24 May Menai Suspension Bridge is badly damaged by fire.

19 June Edward Heath's Conservative Party wins the General Election.

18 July BBC radio sacks Kenny Everett for commenting on a news story about the British Transport Minister's wife passing her driving test.

26-30 August 600,000 people attend the Isle of Wight festival, the largest rock festival ever seen in the UK.

18 September Jimi Hendrix dies in London from a heart attack, aged 27.

23 December The North Tower of the World Trade Centre is topped out at 1,368 ft making it the tallest building in the world.

Top of the Pops

Edison Lighthouse – Love Grows

Elvis Presley – The Wonder Of You

Simon & Garfunkel – Bridge Over Troubled Water

Mungo Jerry – In The Summertime

Dave Edmunds – I Hear You Knocking

What's the unexpected secret that turns their world upside down?

A film for adults to take their children, too!

The Secret Adventures of "The Railway Children"

DINAH SHERIDAN · JENNY AGUTTER · BERNARD CRIBBINS
WILLIAM MERVYN · SALLY THOMSETT · GARY WARREN

memorable movies!

Dressed for success – a beautiful baker's dozen, Miss Liverpool 1971

Crimes of fashion, from funk to punk

The decade that ripped up the rule book

IT IS not for nothing that to many the 1970s are regarded as the years that fashion forgot – hot pants, kipper ties and flares were the hottest fashion of the decade.

While the era got off to a good start, with the hippie look hanging in there and many Liverpudlians still clinging on to their hotpants and minidresses, things sure took a turn for the peculiar from 1973 onwards. No doubt to the disappointment of millions of men, the minidress found itself replaced by the midi, and eventually the floor-skimming maxidress became the must-have cut of choice.

But both sexes were in danger of being arrested by the fashion police when flares hit the stores. The high waist band, patch pocket, mammoth flares made anybody look like a human triangle.

Luckily, fashion designers had thought of a solution and provided us with platform shoes to lift the weight off the floor and ensure

that, on blustery days, your legs were converted into wind tunnels.

Two, three and even four inch stacks became commonplace. And that was just the men!

Neither did women have the monopoly on long hair either in the 70s. As rockbands like Deep Purple and Led Zeppelin stormed the charts, Rapunzel-length locks replaced beehives and bobs and the short back and sides became a thing of the past.

However the glitz and glamour of the disco era did not get to shine for long here on Merseyside as a grim national recession took hold and people became more interested in where their food was coming from than high fashion.

It would in many ways contribute to the birth of one of the most shocking style movements yet – punk – and this was one fashion moment Liverpool was going to make the most of.

Faces Model Agency
arrives in Rodney Street in 1976

Skinheads in 1970

Trendsetters on and off
the pitch – John Toshack
and Kevin Keegan inspect
the Oslo ground

Every city had its punk clubs, but few were as influential as Eric's in Liverpool

Trunk call – no charge for sunbeds here, but the lad on the lilo seems to have run aground

Feeling hot, hot, hot!

Soaring temperatures hit record highs

THERE was only one word to sum up how everyone was feeling in the summer of 1976 ... HOT!

That was the year when the region sweltered like never before. When Meols was warmer than Magaluf and Kirkby was hotter than Kos. And the soaring temperatures didn't last for just a day or two either – the heat went on. And on. And on.

The lack of rain meant the whole country was affected by water rationing.

Gardeners everywhere were forbidden to use hosepipes. By August 24, the situation had become so severe that the government created a new post – Minister for Drought.

With water supplies dwindling, desperate times led to desperate measures and automatic car washing was next to be banned. Having a dirty car suddenly became patriotic. People across the country were told to put bricks or plastic bags full of water in their toilet cisterns to cut down on

the amount of water flushed away. They were also advised to use washing-up water to pour down the toilet instead of flushing.

Everyone was told to bath in less than five inches of water and then re-use it to pour on the garden.

Finally, in September, the heavens opened.

The sight of rain came as a very welcome relief for once – at least for a time. That autumn turned into one of the wettest on record.

Children grabbed the chance
to splash around when Prescot
Road flooded in 1976

Sledge your bets – first past
the post gets an ice cream

Melting snow brought a
minor flood crisis to
Anfield in January 1970

January, 1976 and
workmen struggle
against a freak 85mph
gust to tie down a crane
at Gladstone Branch
Dock, Bootle

CENTRAL STATION GETS THE AXE

IT was the end of the line for a station landmark in 1971.

Workmen with pickaxes and sledgehammers moved in on July 19 to start work demolishing Central Station buildings – a Liverpool landmark since 1874.

The buildings, which had dominated Ranelagh Street for so many years, were being pulled down to make way for the first stages of the city's new underground railway. The new loop line, expected to be up and running within four years, was to link Central Station with James Street, Exchange and Lime Street.

Some argued that its destruction was totally unnecessary and with a bit of imagination the Merseyrail underground station could have been accommodated while the marvellous arched roof was retained to make a covered space for cafes and shop stalls.

But it was not to be. At a prime spot at the junction of Ranelagh Street and Bold Street, the station's plain but attractive Italianate stone facade and fine arched steel and glass roof were bulldozed for eventual replacement by a row of shops.

memorable movies!

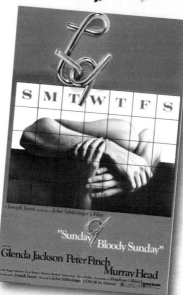

"Sunday, Bloody Sunday"

Glenda Jackson Peter Finch Murray Head

NATIONAL HEADLINES

1 February British Leyland launches the new Morris Marina range of family coupes and saloons, as a direct competitor for the Ford Cortina.

15 February The United Kingdom and Republic of Ireland switch to decimal currency.

28 February Evil Knievel sets a world record, jumping 19 cars.

8 March The British postal workers' strike, led by UPW General Secretary Tom Jackson, ends after 47 days.

27 April Eight members of the Welsh Language Society go on trial for destroying English language road signs in Wales.

23 May Jackie Stewart wins the Monaco Grand Prix.

24 June The Queen officially opens the Kingsway Tunnel.

3 July Jim Morrison, lead singer of The Doors, is found dead in his bathtub in Paris.

15 August The number of British troops in Northern Ireland is raised to 12,500.

Top of the Pops

George Harrison – My Sweet Lord

T-Rex – Hot Love

Diana Ross – I'm Still Waiting

Rod Stewart – Maggie May

Benny Hill – Ernie (The Fastest Milkman In The West)

Not your normal Nine to Five – the Queen on a visit to Merseyrail

The really 'Big Dig'

By Royal Appointment

MERSEYSIDE put on the style to greet the Queen in dazzling sunshine during the summer of 1971, on her visit to open the second Mersey tunnel.

To the delight of the crowd the Queen named the tunnel Kingsway at the historic opening.

She said: "My grandfather named the first Mersey Tunnel in honour of Queen Mary.

"So in honour of my father it is with the greatest pleasure that I declare the second Mersey tunnel open and name it Kingsway."

A big burst of cheering followed from the crowd as the long blue curtains at the tunnel entrance, released by the press of a button by the Queen, fell aside. There above the entrance, carved in Westmorland green stone, was the 31ft long name, each letter covered in gold leaf.

The opening was a colourful yet simple ceremony watched by a 6,000 crowd, including 2,000 schoolchildren, a cross-section of city life.

The Queen was a happy smiling figure when she arrived at the entrance to the tunnel to cheers from a big crowd. Groups of children, many from nearby Scotland Road, whose homes had been affected by the building of the tunnel, waved Union Jacks.

At the tunnel entrance there was a Guard of Honour provided by the First Battalion of the Lancastrian Volunteers.

The Guard of Honour had the Queen's Colour and the Regimental drums gave the Royal salute. The Queen then drove through the tunnel leading a procession of cars, to a welcome at Wallasey by 1,700 excited children. There were also 1,000 members of Wallasey youth organisations.

Hooters blared and lights flashed as the first cars drove through Kingsway after it was opened to the public at midnight.

Crowds emerge from
the Wallasey end of
the tunnel walk

Wirral commuters took
delays in their stride, but
there were few Monday
morning smiles at Central
Low Level, February 14, 1972

Above: The Crosville bus has an opening to the right of the number plate for the conductor to reach up and wind on the destination boards

Ford Escort cars on the production line at the Ford Halewood factory 1972

Above: Traffic queues from Victoria Street towards the Birkenhead tunnel, 1970

CAPRI

Left: The legendary Ford Capri

"This electric bus, battery operated, has ben on trial in Liverpool and other cities," reported the Liverpool Echo in 1972. "Interest in pollution-free electric vehicles is growing."

Air France Concorde sweeps away over the Mersey during a visit in August 1979

Wild times on the Costa del Mersey

Sizzling summers boost a roaring trade

THE 1970s was the decade when the foreign package holiday really came into its own.

Mass tourism invented Madge-orca (where the water don't taste like what it oughta) and helped shape the not altogether satisfying image of Brits abroad.

The promise of guaranteed sunshine in places like Spain meant some people abandoned the British coastline in favour of new destinations.

But in 1976 the hottest summer in 200 years lasted for months and turned the region into Costa Del Merseyside. Sun worshipers flocked to Formby, Ainsdale, West Kirby, Southport, New Brighton and the Isle of Mann beaches to enjoy the unexpectedly warm weather and ice cream sellers did a roaring trade as people did whatever they could to keep cool. Nobody was really sun cream aware so there were burned faces, shoulders and backs everywhere.

Many Brits still looked forward to a slice of holiday camp life at Pontins in Southport or Prestatyn, the setting for the classic 1973 film Holiday On The Buses.

Caravanning holidays were the wheel deal in the Seventies (what better way to spend a weekend than sitting in a tin-box on Formby Point?) while activity and adventure holidays were the new 'in thing' for those following the fitness craze.

You could even take a walk on the wild side after the creation of one of the world's biggest safari parks at Knowsley Hall. The scheme was the brainchild of the then Lord Derby who invested £750,000 into the project.

Sand in your shoes – and the boot, for these Southport visitors

Above: A pride of
lions inspect a visiting
car at Knowsley
Safari Park, July 1972

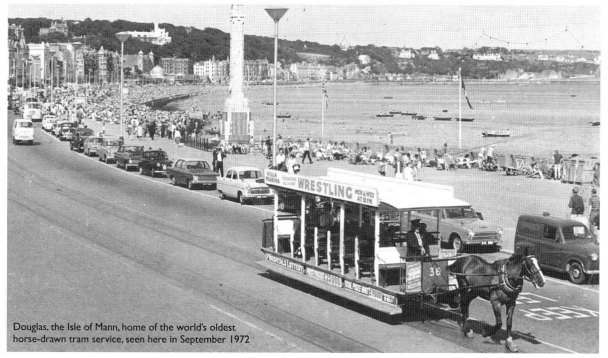

Douglas, the Isle of Mann, home of the world's oldest
horse-drawn tram service, seen here in September 1972

A paddle in Crosby Marina

TOWERING VICTORY FOR ALTON

IT was a meteoric career for David Alton, following his appointment as the country's then youngest councillor in 1972.

At the age of 21, David was elected to Liverpool City Council to represent Low Hill Ward for the Liberals. He swished into big city politics at a time of change. Trevor Jones was embarking on a Liberal revival, which would ultimately crush the Conservative Party while mounting a challenge to Labour.

Young Alton was one of the Jones' boys, promoting 'community politics', an extraordinary idea, which involved the politicians speaking to local people about their worries – from dim street lights to housing co-operatives.

David had passionate beliefs and some were well off the mainstream, but he respected the feelings of others. Life on the council could be hard – once he was almost throttled by an opponent as they debated fair rents.

On another occasion a brick was thrown at him on the street and the wound needed 12 stitches. As he rose to housing chairman and deputy leader of the council, the windows of his house were 'white-washed' by racists who disliked his views on immigration.

From 1979 until 1997, David was a Liberal/Liberal Democrat MP, first in Liverpool Edge Hill and then in the extended constituency of Mossley Hill. In 1997 he became Lord Alton of Mossley Hill and he is now an Independent cross-bench life Peer.

NATIONAL HEADLINES

9 January Coal miners walk out at midnight in their first national strike for almost 50 years.

9 February Prime Minister Ted Heath imposes a three-day week and a state of emergency is declared.

25 February Miners vote in favour for a pay settlement – restrictions on industrial use of electricity end at midnight.

5 June The Duke of Windsor is laid to rest near Windsor Castle. The former King of England passed away on 28 May.

18 June 118 people are killed when a flight from Heathrow to Brussels crashes in Staines, minutes after take-off.

28 July Thousands of British dockers begin an official strike to safeguard jobs.

3 September Mary Peters wins the Pentathlon gold medal at the Munich Summer Olympics. It is a crowning career moment for the Halewood-born athlete, shattering the world record and Olympic record in the process.

6 November The Conservative government freezes pay and prices in an attempt to control spiralling inflation.

Top of the Pops

Nilsson – Without You

Chicory Tip – Son Of My Father

Alice Cooper – School's Out

Chuck Berry – My Ding-A-Ling

Little Jimmy Osmond – Long Haired Lover From Liverpool

memorable movies!

Strike force!

The winter of discontent

THE 1970s were dominated by industrial unrest in Britain and people were fed up with strikes, power cuts and food shortages.

Huge rises in oil prices ultimately led to the three-day week in Britain and 'no power' days. A price of a gallon of petrol leapt from around 36p to 63p.

Industry was hit throughout Merseyside, including Ford at Halewood, Vauxhall at Ellesmere Port and Standard Triumph at Speke.

Strikes and demonstrations dragged drearily on throughout the decade, leading to the Winter of Discontent in 1978/79.

On January 23, 1979, strike chaos gripped the whole of Britain, making it a black Monday for young, old and sick alike. Ambulances ignored emergency calls, hospitals had to stop admissions, schools were forced to close, icy roads were left ungritted, and even gravediggers stopped work in a nation-wide pay protest by local authority workers.

There was also a 24-hour rail strike and a crippling 10-day strike by lorry drivers. Food was running out in Merseyside shops and stores and shelves were empty of basics like sugar, salt, margarine, lard and toilet rolls.

Hospital out-patient clinics were cancelled and 1,400 pensioners in Liverpool went without meals-on-wheels. Schools were closed and buses and trains cancelled. Frustrated motorists abandoned their cars on double yellow lines in the centre of Liverpool as strikes by rail workers and parking attendants brought traffic chaos to the city.

Merseyside also bore the brunt of the lay-offs to hit the North West, with more than 18,000 out of work, including 2,500 at Pilkingtons and 1,200 at AC Delco in Kirkby.

Sugar rush – but only Vesta curry on offer in this shop

Petrol rationing and the queue for coupons at Hanover Street Post Office on the morning of November 23, 1973

Office workers struggle
through the Three Day
Week and 'no power days'

Left: UCATT members
brave the rain on Church
Street, May 1, 1979

Above: Jack Yyden, Liverpool docks'
district chairman of the TGWU,
puts a strike resolution to the vote

The National Union of Seamen, 1970

Marchers arrive at Liverpool Town Hall to protest against the Rent Act, August 1972

Protestors take their campaign to save the ice rink to Liverpool Town Hall, 1979

Men from the Direct Works department picketing at the town hall, March 3, 1976

Above: Women on the march in Liverpool 8 in protest against violence, April 6, 1979

Left: Residents of Buchanan Road, Walton, block the road in protest over traffic from a nearby bakery, following two incidents in which children were injured

TRAGEDY struck the Isle of Man in August 1973, when a blaze at Summerland claimed the lives of 50 people.

The massive £2million fun centre complex in Douglas was reduced to a blackened skeleton as fire swept through it.

The fire started in a small kiosk that fell against the outside of the main building.

Eyewitnesses reported that there was a huge explosion and a tornado of flames took hold. Those who had managed to flee safely reported that emergency doors had been locked and had severely hampered any escape. Summerland was opened on the Douglas waterfront in 1971, designed to accommodate up to 10,000 tourists with a dance area, amusement arcades, restaurants and bars.

The fatal fire in 1973 was the biggest incident that the Isle of Man Fire and Rescue Service has ever dealt with.

On September 3, 1973 the Lieutenant Governor appointed a Commission of Enquiry into the Summerland disaster and the enquiry lasted until February 1974. The Commission urged the immediate revision of Theatre Regulations and drastically changed the whole approach to fire safety on the Isle of Man.

No specific individuals or groups were blamed and the deaths were attributed to misadventure: the delay in evacuation and the flammable building materials were condemned.

memorable movies!

HARRY SALTZMAN and ALBERT R BROCCOLI present
ROGER MOORE as JAMES BOND
IAN FLEMING'S
"LIVE AND LET DIE"
YAPHET KOTTO · JANE SEYMOUR
Produced by HARRY SALTZMAN and ALBERT R BROCCOLI
Directed by GUY HAMILTON · Screenplay by TOM MANKIEWICZ
Title Song Composed by PAUL and LINDA McCARTNEY
and Performed by PAUL McCARTNEY and WINGS
Music Scored by GEORGE MARTIN
United Artists

NATIONAL HEADLINES

1 January The United Kingdom enters the European Economic Community.

26 March Women are admitted to the London Stock Exchange for the first time in the institution's 200 year history.

1 May An estimated 1,600,000 workers in the UK stop work, in support of a Trade Union Congress day of national protest and stoppage against the government's anti-inflation policy.

31 July Militant protestors led by Ian Paisley, disrupt the first sitting of the Northern Ireland Assembly.

26 September Concorde makes its first non-stop crossing of the Atlantic in record-breaking time, flying from Washington to Paris in three hours and 32 minutes.

2 October Tranmere Rovers beat first division superstars Arsenal 1–0 in a League Cup tie.

20 October The spiritual leader of Tibetan Buddhists, the Dalai Lama, visits the UK for the first time.

14 November Princess Anne marries Captain Mark Phillips in Westminster Abbey.

Top of the Pops

Sweet – Blockbuster

Wizzard – See My Baby Jive

Simon Park Orchestra – Eye Level

Gary Glitter – I Love You Love Me Love

Slade – Merry Christmas Everybody

29

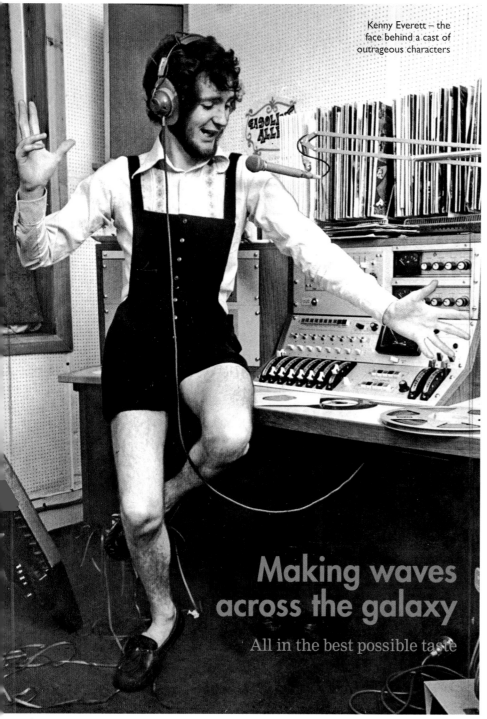

Kenny Everett – the face behind a cast of outrageous characters

Making waves across the galaxy

All in the best possible taste

THE small screen in the 1970s grew up after the innocence of the 1960s.

It became adventurous and was dominated by Merseyside talent. Many Seventies stars established themselves in blockbuster series, classic sit-coms and period dramas.

A Family At War broke out on the telly in 1979, John Finch's 52-part story focused on the upper working class Ashton family in Liverpool. Granada TV appealed to the public to send in their old gas masks, ration books and identity cards and, for added authenticity, the cast had to have wartime haircuts.

Peter Gilmore set sail in The Onedin Line and starred for nine years as the good captain making waves in the ratings. It told the story of a sea dynasty that had its fair share of passion, deceit and skullduggery – both emotional and financial – on the high seas.

Leonard Rossiter, Tom O'Connor, Ken Dodd, Kenneth Cope, Jean Alexander, Alison Steadman, Pauline Daniels, Geoffrey Hughes and Stan Boardman – just a few of the Scouse entertainers who proved to the nation in the 1970s why our reputation for humour was no joke. Not forgetting writer Eddie Braben, who penned the Morecambe and Wise Christmas specials that became an institution during the decade when few British families would ever dream of missing them.

Kenny Everett was the face behind a cast of outrageous characters, a loveable clown who transformed radio with his irreverent and anarchic style. On television, he entertained the nation with his oddball sketches and even provided the "miaows" of a cartoon cat in the "Charley says…" series of public information films.

Radio City, the 'baby' of the airwaves was born on October 21, 1974. It turned Bill Shankly into a chat show host and launched the DJ careers of countless others.

Women in the 70s could relate to Carla Lane's beautifully crafted Butterflies with Wendy Craig. Also a big hit, were the trials and tribulations of Liver Birds Sandra and Beryl (and later Carol) – two young friends sharing a flat in Huskisson Street and a keen interest in parties and men.

The theme tune – performed by The Scaffold – also etched itself into people's memories. Yer dancing? Yer askin'? I'm askin', I'm dancin'." La la la la…..

Peter Gilmore as James Onedin, Anne Stallybrass as his wife and Howard Lang as Baines in The Onedin Line, 1972

Behind the scenes with A Family At War

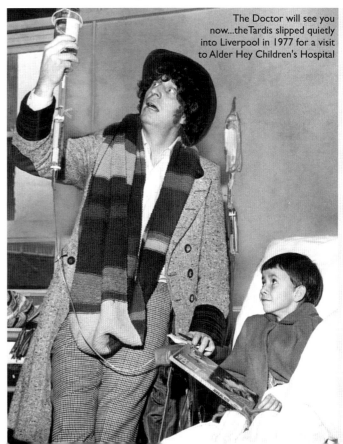

The Doctor will see you now...the Tardis slipped quietly into Liverpool in 1977 for a visit to Alder Hey Children's Hospital

Bill Shankly interviews Harold Wilson in the early days of Radio City

Cooling off in Lime Street before
filming, Liver Bird Liz Estensen with her
flatmate, Nerys Hughes, August 1975

Derek Nimmo was best known for the dotty clerics he played on television, but also hosted Just A Nimmo, pictured here with the Prince of Darkness, Christopher Lee

Below: Freddie Starr was making a great impression in Who Do You Do in 1972

No need to adjust your set – it's Keith Chegwin

Disco inferno – The Real Thing whip the Royal Court crowd into a frenzy

Cum on feel the noize!

Kids go crazy for night fever

IN the 1970s British bands were leading the world, with their spaced-out rock and roll and outrageous stage performances – and they all visited Merseyside to be greeted by sell-out crowds.

In 1971, mass hysteria broke out when T-Rex arrived at the Liverpool Stadium. Other bands that played there included the legendary Led Zeppelin, Dr Feelgood, and Steve Harley and Cockney Rebel. In 1972 an orange-haired David Bowie appeared at the Top Rank with his classic Spiders line-up of Mick Ronson on guitar, Trevor Bolder (bass) and Woody (drums). Elsewhere in the city, the Empire pulled in big names such as Queen and Wings, where fans were moved to tears by Paul McCartney's rendition of Yesterday.

At the heart of the 1970s disco scene in Liverpool was The Real Thing. Singer Eddie Amoo has many fond memories of the era: "There were some great places, I remember some fabulous clubs where you could disco the night away, and they all looked like somebody's front room!

"Places like The Timepiece on Seel Street, the Pun Club in Slater Street, the Sink Club, and the Sportsman.

"Brilliant times were had by all. I think it is the fact that disco was so much fun that made it so successful.

"The clothes were wild in those days, weren't they? But I don't regret it – all the glitter and the platforms, we just loved it."

As glam rock and disco gave way to punk, Eric's Club in Mathew Street ushered in the second wave of the Mersey Sound. After it opened in October 1976, Eric's immediately became the focal point for the city's youth who got to see some of the great cutting-edge punk bands of the time, including The Clash, Iggy Pop, Talking Heads, The Ramones and the Sex Pistols.

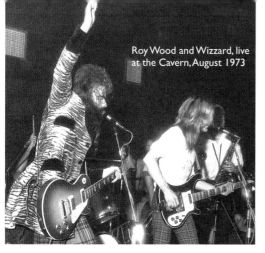
Roy Wood and Wizzard, live at the Cavern, August 1973

All queued up – Eric's was the catalyst for the second wave of the Mersey sound

Our Kid at Whistlers Store, Southport - Brian Farrell, Terry Baccino and Kevin Rowan

Inside The Wooky
Hollow club in 1977

Lighting up with laughter

Spectacular shows pull in the crowds

IN 1977 the Liverpool Echo discussed the rich vein of comedy in the city, suggesting: "The native, natural wit which is inbred in Merseysiders has been one of the shining lights in times of adversity."

It was a time when comedians entertained in cabaret clubs like the famous Shakespeare in Fraser Street – which had the words 'comedy' 'tragedy' and 'music' emblazoned on its frontage – the Wooky Hollow in Anfield and Allinsons in Litherland.

Elsewhere, a Wookiee and his friends had cinema-goers captivated – the Odeon on London Road and the Forum on Lime Street enjoyed glorious box office takings with blockbusters such as Star Wars, Jaws and Superman.

The Odeon was also the scene of religious protests when The Exorcist was released in 1972.

The antics of the Codman family's Punch and Judy show packed out Williamson Square, while in 1971 the first Lord Mayor's Parade brought thousands to watch fifty colourful floats and nine bands set off from King Edward Street.

One of the biggest events for those sizzling Seventies summers was the Liverpool Show at Wavertree Playground. Things began in style, when American astronaut William Anders opened the Liverpool Show in 1971 and was a big hit with the crowds. The Apollo 10 space capsule was on show at an exhibition and it proved to be the centre of attraction. In 1978, the Lord Mayor, Cllr Ruth Dean, arrived in spectacular style in a helicopter. Events in the sun-drenched arena drew in large crowds, and there was a popular wellie-throwing championship. But it was to be the last show of the decade.

Cinema-goers snap up tickets for Jaws at the ABC Forum on Lime Street

These flower girls look blooming lovely, taken at the Lord Mayor's parade, 1971

That's the way to do it! Liverpool Playhouse with Codman's Punch and Judy show in the foreground, January 1973

Thousands flock to enjoy the sunshine
at Liverpool Show during its heyday

The poptastic Tony Blackburn spins some tunes at the Liverpool Show, 1975

A walk in the morning sunshine with Tara...Roma, Toni, Linda and Yvonne

Pam Mayfield of Wallasey fell for Arthur the donkey at Liverpool Show, before he entered the Show Donkey Class – July 15, 1972

An open and shut case? Let's hope not, for the sake of this show streaker

TERROR ATTACKS BRING CARNAGE

1974 proved to be one of the deadliest years in the IRA's mainland bombing campaign.

A total of 38 people were killed in four separate attacks in London, Guilford, Birmingham and on a coach carrying soldiers on the M62.

On February 4, the IRA blew up a coach carrying servicemen and their families on the M62 near Huddersfield. Nine soldiers, a young mother and her two sons died and 38 were injured in the blast.

The coach had been specially commissioned to carry British Army and RAF personnel on leave with their families to several bases, including Catterick, North Yorkshire, during strike action on the trains.

The IRA never claimed responsibility for the terror attack, although Judith Ward, a 25-year-old woman from Stockport, was convicted of 12 counts of murder. However after the police investigation was exposed as flawed, she was released on appeal in 1992.

A memorial to those who lost their lives now stands at Hartshead Moor services.

NATIONAL HEADLINES

7 February Prime Minister Edward Heath calls a general election in an attempt to end the dispute over the miners' strike.

28 February The general election results in an almost dead heat and Harold Wilson becomes Prime Minister again.

10 March Ten miners die in a methane gas explosion at Golborne Colliery near Wigan.

1 April The local government act 1972 comes into force, creating the new Merseyside County, including the boroughs of St Helens and Southport.

6 April Abba win the Eurovision Song Contest for Sweden with 'Waterloo'.

8 August The Watergate scandal forces President Nixon to announce his resignation.

7 November Lord Lucan disappears after the murder of Sandra Rivett, nanny to his children.

Top of the Pops

Terry Jacks – Seasons In The Sun

Carl Douglas – Kung Fu Fighting

David Essex – Gonna Make You A Star

Three Degrees – When Will I See You Again

Mud – Lonely This Christmas

memorable movies!

From the writers of 'Frenzy & Sleuth'
Anthony Shaffer's incredible occult thriller

THE WICKER MAN

Starring
Edward Woodward
Britt Ekland
Diane Cilento
Ingrid Pitt

And
Christopher Lee as Lord Summerisle

Hoppers and choppers
Going like the clackers

THE TR7 may not have been a great success for British Leyland in Speke, but Dinky Toys were still producing them in great numbers in Binns Road in 1978.

Children could buy not only the normal TR7 but also Purdy's version from The New Avengers and even a rally model – although Dinky's biggest seller that year was the Starship Enterprise from Star Trek.

Clackers or Klik-Klacks – two plastic balls on the end of a piece of string – became the craze of the Seventies after being brought back from Spanish beach holidays but ran into controversy amid reports of injured knuckles and the toy's ability to turn into a dangerous missile.

Leaps in technology saw Atari bring blips and bleeps into our homes with electronic ping-pong phenomenon 'Pong'. Musical aficionados could try their prowess out on the stylophone, while wannabe mums could devote all their attention to Tiny Tears.

The coolest bike around had to be the Raleigh Chopper. The high handle bar, high back seated bike proved to be an instant hit and everybody just had to have one. If you needed a more energetic mode of transport then what about a Spacehopper? The bright orange ball with the face of a kangaroo and two horn shaped handles would just about get you down to the shops for a quarter of Everton Mints or Mojo Fruits.

Shoot! was read by hundreds of thousands of football crazy youngsters, all desperate to learn what their footballing heroes got up to in their spare time.

Shoot! was known for its star columnists and guest writers – in 1978 Ray Clemence thoughtfully reveals: "A taxi took me to North London where after a late dinner, I joined the rest of the England squad, which included my former Liverpool team-mate Kevin Keegan, who had also had an eventful day launching his range of sportswear."

Busy packing the mountain of toys for the Lord Mayor's Christmas toy appeal, December 20, 1974

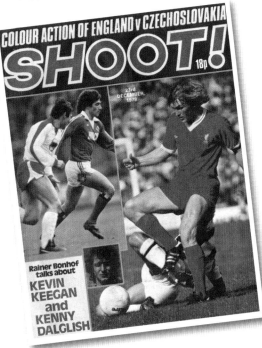

The TR7 speeds off the production line at the Meccano factory

Goodbye Billy Bunter

Hello Grange Hill...

UNEMPLOYMENT was rearing its ugly head as the 70s arrived.

This time for Scouse school kids. Many milk monitors lost their jobs. In 1971 councils were furious at the School's Minister, Margaret Thatcher, who decided to end free school milk for the over sevens.

It earned her the nickname 'Thatcher, Thatcher Milk Snatcher'. And the pupils weren't too kind either.

Happily there was a mould-breaking education system available for those Liverpudlians who missed out on university or simply didn't want to leave the city and prefer to study (and drink) at home. The OU Open University saw its first student applications and by the middle of 1970 there were enough to make it viable. In January 1971 the rookie students began work on their first foundation courses.

As comprehensive schools grew throughout the city and the country, one lad had already left such an established institution clearly inspired by his own experiences in Liverpool.

Huyton-born Phil Redmond, ex of St Kevin's in Kirkby, would change the way everyone perceived education with his mould-breaking TV series Grange Hill, an idea he came up with in 1975 and which hit the screens three years later.

Phil, a one-time quantity surveyor turned prolific screenwriter, sold it to BBC1. The programme was about an inner city school set in fictitious Northam, but despite a lack of Scouse accents everyone believed it was based on a Liverpool school. It was the first time the playground and classroom was reflected the way it actually was in real life. They had real nicknames, too. The teachers were learning about life just as much as the kids. Bike sheds, bullying, and sex – Phil's no-holds-barred concept would run for nearly three decades inspiring many adult school dramas to follow. "Crikey and cripes!" said the TV critics at the time, Billy Bunter of Greyfriars is no more.

A fractured gas main and school evacuation made it a swinging day for pupils from the Dingle Vale wing of Shorefields Comprehensive, September 19, 1974

April 7, 1972: The Liverpool Echo asks "What sort of jobs wait for our children when they finally leave school?"

Come on – you know how Greensleeves goes

Above: Teenagers from the St John's Estate in Huyton rock around the clock – for a few hours at least – at a community centre dance in 1977

Left: Just add a little drop of...BOOM!

Above: Youngsters from
Litherland Moss Infants'
School meet the road safety
mascot, Tufty, in January, 1972

Right: The Keep Britain
Tidy boys from
Quarry Bank School,
Liverpool Show, 1975

A party of schoolboys and staff
depart Lime Street Station for a 10-
day holiday at Emmetten, Switzerland

The scene never changes, only the fashions and cars mark the passing years on Oxton Street in the shadow of Goodison Park

IRA JAILED IN WATERLOO RAID

FIVE IRA terrorists were jailed for life in 1975 after a terror campaign ended with a siege in Waterloo.

Twenty-five detectives armed with handguns went to the house in Oxford Road, Waterloo on July 10. Detective Sergeant Thomas Davies shouted at the dawn raid: "Open the door, police!"

He recalled later: "I heard the sound of voices in the flat. The door didn't move. There was a bang and a hole appeared in the door and I got a bullet in my stomach."

After they surrendered, the terrorists were found to have 458lbs of explosives, 168 detonators and several booby trap devices.

They were jailed for life at Manchester Crown Court.

Det Sgt Davies had a bullet lodged in his spine, but made a remarkable recovery and was discharged from Walton Hospital a month later, resuming police duties six months later. The following year he was awarded the Queen's Gallantry Medal and a total of 19 Merseyside officers were given Merit Badges for their roles in the Waterloo incident.

NATIONAL HEADLINES

11 February Margaret Thatcher defeats Edward Heath to become the first woman leader of the Conservative Party.

13 February British mineworkers' leaders agree to a 35% pay rise from the coal board.

4 March Silent film legend Charlie Chaplin becomes Sir Charles at Buckingham Palace, after being knighted in the New Year's Honours List.

30 April The Vietnam war ends as Saigon surrenders to North Vietnamese forces.

9 June The UK votes yes in a referendum to stay in the European Community.

15 August The Birmingham Six are sentenced (wrongly) to life imprisonment.

22 September IRA bombings across Northern Ireland places the ceasefire it declared seven months ago in serious doubt.

1 October Muhammad Ali defeats Joe Frazier in the boxing 'Thrilla in Manila'.

11 December Tension in the Cod War grows as an Icelandic gunboat opens fire on British fishery support vessels in the North Atlantic Sea.

Top of the Pops

Status Quo – Down Down

Tammy Wynette – Stand By Your Man

David Bowie – Space Oddity

Bay City Rollers – Bye Bye Baby

Queen – Bohemian Rhapsody

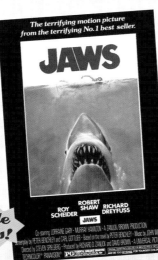

The terrifying motion picture from the terrifying No. 1 best seller.

JAWS

ROY SCHEIDER · ROBERT SHAW · RICHARD DREYFUSS

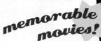
memorable movies!

49

Liverpool players Jimmy Case, Phil Neal and Terry McDermott celebrate after winning the 1977 European Cup Final

A decade of records

Golden goals for legends red and blue

AFTER dismantling a side that had won the League championship twice and the FA Cup in successive seasons, Liverpool manager Bill Shankly rebuilt a team of comparative youngsters, all with great skill.

Kevin Keegan was an instant hit; he had speed, skill, courage and the ability to score goals. Shankly's successor Bob Paisley signed Kenny Dalglish from Celtic for £440,000 and he also became an Anfield legend. He had an immediate impact, scoring 30 goals in his first season and hit the winning goal in the European Cup Final against FC Bruges.

Liverpool moved across Europe like a colossus, collecting championships, UEFA Cups, FA Cups and European Cups to become the unchallenged kings of the continent. In 1977 the romantic city of Rome witnessed the climax of an unforgettable football season when Liverpool played Borussia Moenchengladbach, with the European Cup as the prize. That same year there was Liverpool's victorious run-in to the League Championship, the FA Cup Final at Wembley, the top-quality semi-final at Maine Road, and the last-gasp drama of Everton's League Cup series with Aston

Villa. At Goodison, Everton had started the decade in style by winning the League Championship in 1970. The Seventies Blues were known as the Mersey Millionaires, a nickname well suited. In February 1974, they smashed the British transfer record to lure Birmingham City's prolific goalscorer Bob Latchford to Goodison Park.

Everton certainly got their money's worth and Latchford regularly topped their goalscoring chart. In 1977-78 he was the first player in the top division for six years to net 30 League goals – claiming a £10,000 prize from a national newspaper for doing so.

Bob Latchford –
Everton's top scorer for
six successive seasons

Above: Everton
celebrate a 1-0
victory over
Liverpool in the
1978 derby

Right: Andy
King, who
scored the 25-
yarder goal,
that ended
seven years of
Everton derby
agony at
Goodison

Putting a shine on the silverware – that's Everton's Lillie Pipkin

Left: This policeman's having a ball, as Liverpool fans celebrate winning the 1978 European Cup

Right: May 1973 – Shanks and the boys show off the UEFA Cup, the First Division Trophy and the Central League Trophy, while John Conteh holds his Lonsdale belt

LIVER POOL
F. C.

SPECIAL

186

53

Red Rum wins the 1974 Grand National, to the delight of his Head Lad, Jackie Granger

Rummy the wonder horse

Triple win for the marvel of Merseyside

RED Rum, Merseyside's own wonder horse, made history on April 2, 1977, when he became the first horse to win the Grand National three times.

The nation's favourite four-legged friend crossed the line at Aintree a full 25 lengths from Churchtown Boy. Rummy not only finished the gruelling four-and-a-half mile race five times in a row, but had won it three times and finished second twice. He had jumped a total of 150 great Aintree fences without once falling. The historic hat-trick was a triumph for the courage of both Red

Rum and Ginger McCain who had lovingly looked after him and brought out his best.

Liverpool Stadium enjoyed its greatest night when John Conteh successfully defended his World light-heavyweight title against Lenny Hutchins. Conteh won the WBC light-heavyweight crown in October 1974 at Wembley, outpointing Argentinean Jorge Ahumada after 15 rounds. Successful defences came, first against American Lonnie Bennet, and then in Copenhagen against Mexican Yaqui Lopez before Conteh's most memorable performance.

He returned home on March 5 1977 to halt American Len Hutchings at the Liverpool Stadium, on one of the most celebrated nights in the city's illustrious fight history.

At Royal Birkdale in 1971 it was the year of the game's greatest entertainer, Lee Trevino. Defending champion Jack Nicklaus and British favourite Tony Jacklin were among the big guns at Birkdale that year, but the in-form Trevino loomed large as a major threat. A birdie four at the last gave 'Supermex' a 278 to win the Open by one shot.

Left: 1971 Open Championship winner, Lee Trevino proves a big hit with the Royal Birkdale crowd

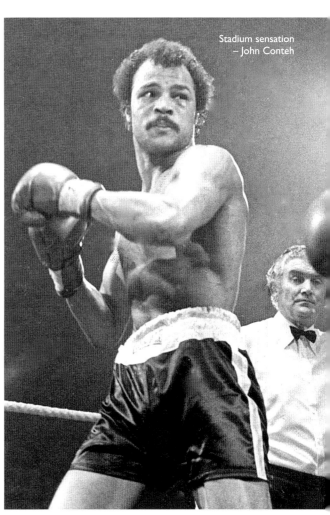

Stadium sensation – John Conteh

Red Rum is greeted by jubillant supporters after winning the 1973 Grand national

Blood, sweat and tears

When passion
turns to violence

AS recently as the mid 1960s, it was not unknown for home and away supporters to exchange scarfs as they swapped ends at half time.

However by the early 1970s a significant number of fans were more likely to be exchanging punches than pleasantries.

Though even then most supporters were only interested in watching the football, the "barmy armies", who had started to take the tribal divides inherent in the game a stage too far, were having their moment.

The ordinary fan, as the non-hooligan became known, seemed powerless to prevent the mayhem often acted out in their name while the football authorities, egged on by "hang them, flog them" supporters in Westminster and Fleet Street, lacked the vision to confront hooliganism and football's overall Victorian squalor, head-on.

Instead they erected perimeter fences simply to confine the problem to the terraces and prayed it would just go away.

As it got worse, the further entrenched response was to build higher, uglier and desperately more dangerous barriers.

Some of the fanzines around at the time had warned of the dangers of fences, though nobody predicted the scale of the catastrophe to come.

DISCO FEVER SWEEPS THE NATION

THE Seventies were the glory days for Toxteth soul stars The Real Thing and in 1976 they found themselves alongside a host of Liverpool bands scoring chart success.

'You To Me Are Everything' spent three weeks at Number 1 in June and was the first single by a black British band to top the singles chart. Written by Ken Gold and Michael Denne and produced by Ken Gold, it was the band's sole number one single in the UK. Ten years later it became the first single to make the Top Ten in original and remixed forms.

Back in 1976, Liverpool band Our Kid scored a Number 2 with 'You Just Might See Me Cry', Liverpool Express made Number 9 with 'You Are My Love', Buster made Number 49 with 'Sunday' while Supercharge achieved chart success in Australia with 'You've Gotta Get Up And Dance'.

One of the most memorable gigs of the decade was when Elton John brought the Captain Fantastic Tour to the Liverpool Empire in 1976. That night, Liverpool FC were playing away at Wolves and if they won, they won the League. During the guitar solo on 'Saturday Night's Alright For Fighting', he went off stage. The roar that went up when he came back five minutes later with a big board reading Liverpool 3 Wolves 1 was deafening.

memorable movies!

EVERY YEAR BRINGS A GREAT MOVIE. EVERY DECADE A GREAT MOVIE MUSICAL!

NATIONAL HEADLINES

7 January British and Icelandic ships clash at sea in the Cod War.

16 March Harold Wilson resigns as Prime Minister, stating that he intends to remain on the backbench of the Commons in an advisory role but would not interfere with government decisions.

3 April The Eurovision Song Contest is won by the UK, represented by Brotherhood Of Man with the song 'Save All Your Kisses For Me'.

5 April James Callaghan becomes the new Prime Minister.

20 June Czechoslovakia beats West Germany on penalties to win Euro 1976.

3 July The great British heatwave reaches its peak, with temperatures reaching 35.9 degrees Celsius.

20 July America's Viking I spacecraft lands on Mars, beaming back to Earth the first photographs of the planet's surface.

1 December The Sex Pistols appear on Bill Grundy's television show, shocking viewers with four-letter expletives.

Top of the Pops

Pussycat – Mississippi

Elton John & Kiki Dee – Don't Go Breaking My Heart

Showaddywaddy – Under The Moon Of Love

Abba – Dancing Queen

Johnny Mathis – When A Child Is Born

Where's me Giro?

The symbol of a new world

ONE of the most famous and biggest employers in the 1970s was National Giro.

They even reluctantly gave birth to a phrase that spread across Merseyside and across the country: "Where's me Giro?"

The name came from the payment cheque for those on the dole. The Giro was processed in Bootle's Bridle Road nine-storey glass Centre at the National Giro HQ which was opened by the then Postmaster General Tony Benn in 1969.

It was a symbol of a brave new world on the eve of the '70s when Liverpool industry – manufacturing and commercial – was going through momentous changes. 'The Giro' as it was affectionately called looked like a hospital, but was the clinical heart of the Post Office's aims to have its very own bank.

In the Sefton region many school leavers not opting for further education signed up for this organisation and rose through the civil service in the process. The Company even published its own newspaper. In 1978 National Giro renamed itself national Girobank. Girobank was, however, always plagued by reports of closure from an incoming Tory government. It was eventually taken over by Alliance and Leicester in the 90s.

Over in Speke, Liverpool Airport was taken over by the Merseyside Development Corporation. One of its many star guests was Concorde which made the first of many visits in 1979.

Tate and Lyle's was a sweet success and a big employer. Like most factory workers their staff always liked to have a good night out on pay day in the city centre clubs.

T & L's girls had distinctive bib and braces overalls or "dungies" as they were called. In the '70s you could spot many of them going into town after their 2-10 shift.

And there was many a tear from everyone who grew up with a Meccano set. After brief periods of resurgent prosperity in the 50s and a series of takeovers in later decades, production at the world famous Binns Road Factory ended in 1979. The doors were finally bolted using the best rivets available.

A busy scene inside the Giro building – 1975

The first meeting of Merseyside County Council in May 1973, led by Councillor Bill Sefton

Left: Private Harry 'Tommy Cooper' Kemp of West Kirby, a favourite with the Derry boys who visit the car park command post

Right: Sweets being stuffed in a container at Barker and Dobson's, en route for sweet toothed New Yorkers

The biggest cold store in the region –
Seaforth Dock frozen by the weather and the
lorry drivers' strike in January 1979

Boxing clever

Cargo revolution ends a labour of love

FOR so long, Liverpool and Birkenhead docks had expanded and thrived as they faced the New World.

Suddenly, as Europe became more pre-eminent and Great Britain as a former imperial Asiatic power waned in its influence, the Merseyside docks were facing in the wrong direction on the wrong coast.

Liner passengers would take off for the airlines and cargo – previously handled as break-bulk loads with its need for cargo ships and their familiar forest of derricks and labour-intensive workforce – would be

felled by containerisation. In the 1970s, the Mersey Docks and Harbour Board was hit by a financial crisis.

The board was still struggling with working methods devised decades earlier and had not adapted to the technical changes in the maritime industry.

Staring bankruptcy in the face, the board promoted an Act of Parliament which led to the setting up of the Mersey Docks and Harbour Company in 1971. That move, coupled with the building of the £50m development at Seaforth, gave the new

company a fighting chance of survival.

Serenaded by ships' sirens, a maroon and jets of water from an escorting salvage vessel, Blue Star Line's meat ship Tasmania Star became the first ship to use the new £50 million Seaforth dock development in December 1971.

The sheer volume of Seaforth's sprawling acres of mud and rubble tended to dwarf all else during a ceremony that was deliberately set in a low key to emphasise the practical rather than spectacular nature of the occasion.

The first container lorries arrive at Seaforth on May 2, 1972 – Pat Breen of Blenheim Street, Liverpool, made a bit of history by driving in the first vehicle

Below: The Control Room of the Liverpool Grain Terminal, 1976

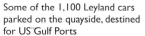

Some of the 1,100 Leyland cars parked on the quayside, destined for US Gulf Ports

Blue Star Line's meat
ship Tasmania Star,
becomes the first ship
to use the new
Seaforth dock
development in 1971

EVERTON'S LONG PLAYING RECORD

GORDON Lee's four-year spell as Everton manager is often unfairly described as a failure – in his first season in 1977 the team finished ninth and reached the League Cup Final and the FA Cup semi-finals.

"Everton's Long Playing Record," was the Liverpool Echo's header on Thursday, March 19, 1977 – after Bob Latchford's close range goal in the final minute at Hillsborough ensured it was the first ever domestic cup final to go to three matches. While it was an historic moment, the newspaper's Charles Lambert reflected on the bond the Blues' cup run was helping to forge with their fans.

"This League Cup Final, this incredible story of sweat and effort and some of the most committed tackling I have ever seen, is the vehicle through which Everton are forming a communion with their supporters," he reported.

"There is a new spirit on the terraces – and in the stands, too, for last night the chant of 'Everton are magic' a chant which looks like becoming their new theme song, came from the stands as much as from the other parts of the ground."

After a prohibitively expensive week – a trip to Wembley on the Saturday then a hastily arranged trip to Hillsborough four days later – the Blues entertained Derby County in the quarter-finals of the FA Cup another three days after that, in front of 42,409 fans.

Goals from Bob Latchford and Jim Pearson ensured that the love affair with the fans continued – then on the Tuesday another 56,000 crammed into Goodison for a goalless derby match. But the Blues' hopes of lifting the League Cup were dashed as they lost the second replay to Villa 3-2 after extra time. It was an era when Everton regularly suffered the cruellest luck.

memorable movies!

A long time ago in a galaxy far, far away...

STAR WARS

NATIONAL HEADLINES

20 January Jimmy Carter becomes the 39th President of the United States.

27 March A collision between KLM and PanAm Boeing 747s in Tenerife kills 583 people, the worst single aviation accident on record.

2 April Red Rum wins the Grand National for the third time.

27 May The Sex Pistols release the single 'God Save The Queen'.

21 June Crowds greet the Queen in Liverpool as she visits the city for her Silver Jubilee tour.

1 July Virginia Wade beats Betty Stöve in the Wimbledon final to claim the title. It is her sixteenth appearance at Wimbledon.

16 August Elvis Presley is found dead at Graceland.

14 November Firefighters go on the first ever National Strike.

27 December Star Wars is screened in British cinemas for the first time.

Top of the Pops

Donna Summer –
I Feel Love

David Soul –
Silver Lady

Hot Chocolate –
So You Win Again

Elvis Presley –
Way Down

Wings –
Mull Of Kintyre

The Queen stops to meet
some of her fans

Crowning moment for Jubilee year

Street parties rejoice at Silver celebrations

IT has to be a very special reason to invite the Queen and in the 1970s, Merseyside secured three magnificent and memorable Royal visits.

As well as launching the Kingsway tunnel in 1971 and attending the official opening of Liverpool Cathedral in 1978, the Queen and Duke of Edinburgh delighted crowds for the Silver Jubilee celebrations in 1977.

Hundreds of thousands turned out in glorious sunshine to line the roads with a colourful sea of red, white and blue, and cheered and waved flags all along the Royal route through the heart of Merseyside.

After planting a silver birch tree at St Helens, the Queen with the Duke left for Liverpool and a full programme of events. All police leave was cancelled for the big day and more than 150 buses took 17,000 school children to Hope Street, Liverpool, for one of the highlights of the Royal tour – a musical feast of colour and song, most of it in the open air.

The Archbishop of Liverpool, the Most Rev Derek Worlock, escorted the Royal couple into the Metropolitan Cathedral for the first of eight scenes of a musical tableau that stretched all along Hope Street.

At Liverpool Cathedral, the Bishop of Liverpool, the Right Rev David Sheppard, waited for the Queen and Duke for the final scene of the pageant.

At Gladstone Lock the Royal couple were piped aboard the Royal Iris, the Mersey ferryboat chosen as the Queen's flagship for a review of shipping in the area. A Royal salute at the Liverpool landing stage preceded the party boarding the Royal Yacht Britannia tied up at the stage to prepare for a glittering private reception on board later. 1977 was the Queen's year – and the whole nation celebrated her 25 years on the throne.

A Jubilee street party in
Pilch Lane, Knotty Ash

I wanna be in charge!
Big ambitions for
these youngsters

Mark Moore of Fincham Green,
Huyton, 'shows the flag' in a big way

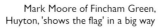

65

Above: Children in front of Liverpool Cathedral dance for the Queen

Bootle residents get in the spirit of the Silver Jubilee celebrations

Britannia arrives on the
River Mersey

An itch for kitsch

Living the digital dream

THE 1970s was a decade of innovation – the watch industry swung to the LED (Light Emitting Diode) and digital watches became the fad of the decade.

Pocket calculators and Polaroid cameras became popular, and a key status symbol was one of the new-fangled Betamax video recorders.

Shag carpets, beanbag chairs and lava lamps adorned every groovy '70s lounge. Freezer ownership rocketed and appliances were no longer just white, but came in affluent colours like Avocado Green and Harvest Gold.

In Seventies suburbia the drinks party was alive and well. The Hostess trolley was the must-have for entertaining and guests would no doubt be offered a prawn cocktail, steak garni, Black Forest gateau or gin and tonic – "Another little top-up Ange?"

Home-brew became more and more popular as the economy hit the wall, when one corner of the kitchen had more bottles, flasks and tubing than a mad professor's laboratory.

It was the decade of the advertising slogan: "Martini – Anytime, anyplace, anywhere", "American Express? – That'll do nicely Sir", "Nice one Cyril, let's av another one!"

The Cinzano ads saw the unforgettable pairing of Leonard Rossiter and Joan Collins performing 30-second masterpieces of comedy. Rossiter's oblivious oaf would always find a way to inadvertently throw his drink over the straight-laced lady-of-society, Melissa.

1970s man was irresistible though thanks to the heady fragrance of Hai Karate. The wacky television adverts, starring the beautiful and bosomy Valerie Leon, had the effect of increasing the sales of this aftershave considerably, as well as the blood pressure of the male population.

Above: Showing off her true colours amid some dazzling designs – Seventies woman is quite the social chameleon

How thrilled we were to get a Betamax video recorder – until VHS swept the market

Left: Drinking partners Lawrie Barker and Alan Shellard raise their glasses to DIY beer

Above: A campaign run by Ugden's tobacco firm, aimed at getting women to smoke pipes

Leonard Rossiter once again manages to drench Joan Collins with his Cinzano straight-laced lady-of-society, Melissa.

'No go' zone gets the green light

But stores foot the cost

MARCH 18, 1974 was the day Liverpool's main shopping street changed forever – it was dubbed "the biggest traffic shut down in living memory".

From that date the busy thoroughfare was closed to traffic, as work started on "one of the biggest pedestrian precincts in Britain, stretching from Paradise Street to Bold Street and from Whitechapel to Williamson Square."

A corporation spokesman told the Liverpool Echo: "The purpose is to improve dramatically the safety, comfort and enjoyment of shoppers."

But just a couple of days after work began, the pedestrianisation was dismissed as being "half-baked and half-hearted".

In its editorial comment, the Liverpool Echo said: "People from all over Merseyside are confused and bewildered by the changes that have befallen Liverpool city centre this week.

"The shock has been considerable and has affected many people psychologically, leaving them almost breathless by the roadside at the scale of it all."

And six months after cars and buses had given way to trees and benches, store bosses were still divided in their opinions. "We have lost many of our former customers, because half the buses that used to pass the store now take another route," said a spokesman for Lewis's.

Brandon Henry, general manager of George Henry Lee and chairman of the Liverpool Stores Committee, said: "The stores in the centre of the pedestrian area can find no fault with it" – but he felt those on the periphery were not happy…

Church Street, March 18, 1974 – its first full day without traffic

Decimal currency makes its debut in Lewis's

Above: Coopers' Church Street store, which ground its last coffee bean on March 11, 1972

Left: A customer of butcher Benny Chambers in Williamson Square chooses a Christmas turkey

An Atlantean leads
a bus convoy up
Parker Street

THE CHAMPIONS OF EUROPE

LIVERPOOL'S first European Cup Final victory in 1977 was the catalyst for the most astonishing run of silverware collected in English football history.

The next battle came on home soil just 12 months later when the Bruges team arrived at Wembley to test Liverpool's mettle as title-holders. Thankfully, Liverpool had perhaps the finest tactical mind of them all in Paisley and the canny Geordie was able to mastermind another victory that confirmed the Reds' status as Europe's most powerful outfit.

If Bob Paisley's 1977-78 side was a team in transition – both Dalglish and Souness had been recruited to replace Anfield idols like Kevin Keegan and Ian Callaghan – it was a swift shift. The new boys combined to land the European Cup at Wembley in May 1978,

then the following season dominated the top division like no other side had ever done before.

As the First Division challengers lined up to try and knock them off their perch, Liverpool sent out a message that they were there to stay. Terry McDermott scored Liverpool's seventh goal against Spurs on September 4, 1978, their biggest league win since World War II – a record which stood for a further 12 years. It was an afternoon of sun-drenched splendour at Anfield in a season of records.

NATIONAL HEADLINES

13 February Anna Ford becomes the first female newsreader on ITN.

30 March The Conservative Party recruits advertisers Saatchi & Saatchi to win votes, ahead of the General Election.

1 May May Day becomes a bank holiday for the first time.

1 June The 1978 FIFA World Cup kicks off in Argentina – the host country also won the competition. England had failed to qualify.

19 June Ian Botham becomes the first man in the history of cricket to score a century and take 8 wickets in 1 inning of a Test match.

25 July Louise Brown, the world's first 'test-tube baby', is born in Oldham.

16 October Pope John Paul II succeeds Pope John Paul I, after only 33 days of papacy. John Paul I had succeeded Pope Paul VI but died on 28 September.

25 October The Queen is greeted by crowds in Liverpool, at a service of thanksgiving and dedication to mark the completion of Liverpool Cathedral.

Top of the Pops

Kate Bush – Wuthering Heights

Commodores – Three Times A Lady

Bee Gees – Night Fever

John Travolta & Olivia Newton-John – You're The One That I Want

Boney M – Mary's Boy Child

John Travolta Olivia Newton-John

GREASE is the word

memorable movies!

"It was like this when we sat down, honest"

The future's in our sites

Toast of the town or just taking the piste?

THROUGH economic ups and downs, communities retained their fighting spirit.

On the outskirts of the city new homes were built and the next stage of slum clearances began. Families in the north – Scotland Road, Everton and Vauxhall – were generally moved to Kirkby and Cantril Farm, and in the south people were re-housed in Speke and Netherley.

"There was a good deal of sentimental regret a few years back when the dilapidated but picturesque streets in the heart of Liverpool came down to make way for St John's Precinct," wrote the Liverpool Echo in April 1970.

"But some of the modern buildings that replace them are acquiring a character of their own and a decidedly local one at that."

In 1973, the Daily Post & Echo moved to Old Hall Street, into new £8.8m headquarters which incorporated some of the world's most advanced thinking, both in the design of the building itself and the equipment it housed.

It took 10,500 concrete blocks to build the new 17-storey Royal Insurance UK head office building in Old Hall Street. On May 5, 1973, the topping out ceremony was performed at 290 feet – the Royal Insurance flag and that of the contractors was

unfurled and the 300 workmen employed on the project traditionally toasted the building with pints of beer.

But best laid plans went downhill for Kirkby in 1975, when a scheme to create an artificial ski slope was shelved and thousands of pounds wasted.

At 410ft long and 70ft wide, the outdoor slope dominated the town's skyline. But after a series of disasters including vandalism and 'bubbles' on the surface, the problem pile was abandoned.

Costs for the troubled project had soared to £114,000 leading to it being branded 'Britain's most expensive pile of dirt'.

An aerial view of the wasteland bordering Everton Road, September 1975

The beginning of the end. Going.....

....going...

Gone!

The skyline in 1977 – the Liverpool Echo and Daily Post building, the Royal Insurance mammoth, St John's Beacon and the Atlantic Tower Hotel

Dominating the Kirkby skyline in April 1974, the artificial ski slope in Bewley Road, later to be known as 'Britain's most expensive pile of dirt'

A roof with a view from 290 feet: the topping out ceremony of the Royal Insurance UK head office building, May 1973

"Who would want to live in this monstrosity?" asked one Liverpool Echo reader in 1975. The North Western Hotel on Lime Street

78

Nearing completion in April, 1971, Liverpool's St George's Hotel and St John's Market

A view rom the Silver Jubilee road bridge of Viaduct Street's terrace, looking down to Mersey View in West Bank, Widnes, flanked by the Queen Aethelflaeda Railway Bridge – July 1973

FIRE SWEEPS THROUGH ST JOHN'S

FIRE broke out at Liverpool's showpiece shopping centre, St John's Precinct, in December 1979, causing £8m worth of damage.

The entire market area in the Precinct was devastated as the fire, caused by an electrical fault, swept through the stalls fanned by 90mph wind. Firefighters evacuated 850 people from the Precinct. Ten shops, just starting their busiest week of the year, were reduced to charred shells. Many more were damaged.

About one-third of the roof inside the market was destroyed. The fire caused chaos for the market traders – but they shrugged off the cold in Williamson Square to keep their customers satisfied.

memorable movies!

NATIONAL HEADLINES

22 January Public workers across the country strike in what is to become known as the Winter of Discontent.

28 March James Callaghan's government loses a motion of confidence by one vote, forcing a general election.

31 March The Royal Navy withdraws from Malta.

4 May The Conservatives win the general election and Margaret Thatcher becomes the first female Prime Minister of Britain.

17 July Athlete Sebastian Coe sets a new record for running a mile, completing it in 3 minutes 48.95 seconds.

27 August Lord Mountbatten and three others are assassinated by the Provisional Irish Republican Party.

2 September Police discover a woman's body in an alleyway near Bradford city centre – it is the 12th victim of the mysterious Yorkshire Ripper.

Top of the Pops

Gloria Gaynor – I Will Survive

Tubeway Army – Are Friends Electric?

Blondie – Heart Of Glass

Boomtown Rats – I Don't Like Mondays

Pink Floyd – Another Brick In The Wall

Other publications from
Trinity Mirror NW²

Wild Merseyside
£4.99+
FREE P+P UK only

**Macca, the Saint and
the Screen Goddess**
£8.99+
Free P+P UK only

**The New Age
of Steam**
£4.99+
£1.50 P+P UK only

Street Stars
£14.99+
Free P+P UK only

Mersey Mastermind
£8.99+
Free P+P UK only

**The Great
Liverpool Pub Crawl**
£8.99+
Free P+P UK only

Talk like the Scousers
£8.99+
Free P+P UK only

Dummy Bullets
£6.99+
Free P+P UK only

Visit www.merseyshop.com or call 0845 143 0001
Monday to Friday 9am-5pm

Trinity Mirror NW²

Trinity Mirror North West & North Wales
PO Box 48, Old Hall Street, Liverpool L69 3EB

Trinity Mirror Sports Media Executive Editor
Ken Rogers